FIRST PETS

Gerbils

Kate Petty

BARRON'S

Gerbils as pets

The first pet gerbils came from the Mongolian desert where they live in underground burrows. They have long tails and strong hind legs, like tiny kangaroos. Some rodent pets, such as hamsters and mice, wake up at night, but gerbils like to play in the daytime. They are fun to keep and easy to tame. Gerbils live for three to four years.

Mongolian gerbil in its natural home

Young Mongolian gerbil ▷

All sorts of gerbils

Most pet gerbils are "agoutis," which are the same sandy color as wild gerbils. But you can buy them in other colors. There are black ones, white ones, and beautiful silvery-gray varieties. A few pet shops sell Egyptian gerbils. They are smaller than Mongolian gerbils but make equally good pets.

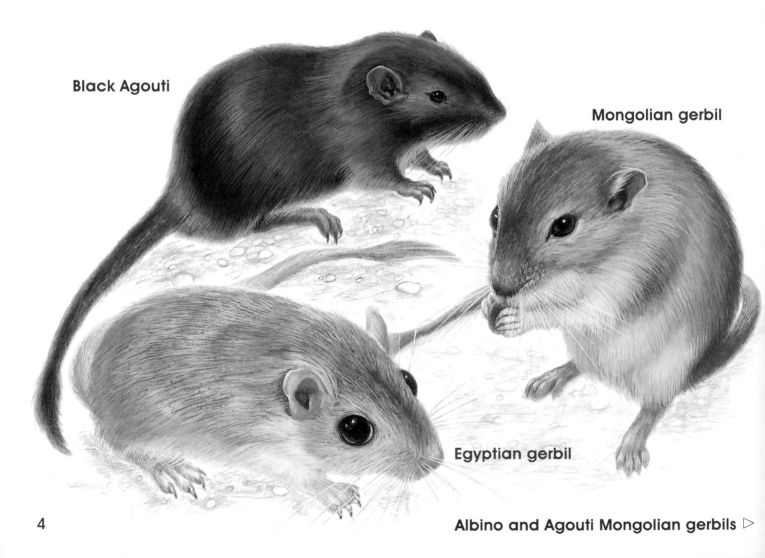

Black Agouti

Mongolian gerbil

Egyptian gerbil

Albino and Agouti Mongolian gerbils ▷

A closer look

A male gerbil is about 4 inches (10 cm) high and weighs about 4 1/2 ounces (130 g). Females are smaller – almost 3 inches (7 cm). Their long, fur-covered tails help them to balance. If an enemy pounces on the tail, the fur comes off and the gerbil escapes. The fur never grows back. Gerbils can see all around with their large eyes and have good hearing.

The fur-covered tail of this white gerbil is quite different from the tail of a mouse or a hamster.

Gerbils have large, bright eyes and long whiskers. ▷

Jumpers

Gerbils are fantastic jumpers. Their back legs are extra strong, and they can leap away from danger very quickly. They can even manage a vertical takeoff. Pet gerbils are very nimble and are hard to catch if they escape. Gerbils stand up on their hind legs to get a better view of their surroundings.

Gray Agouti gerbil jumping

A gerbil stretched to its full height to take a look around ▷

Eating

Pet gerbils need to be fed only once a day. They eat a mixture of grains and enjoy a few dandelion leaves or fresh vegetables. A carrot or a piece of wood to gnaw on keeps their teeth from growing too long. Although gerbils are desert animals and need very little to drink, they must always have a supply of fresh water.

A feast for a lilac gerbil includes grains, seeds, hay, fresh fruit and vegetables, and some raisins.

Egyptian gerbil keeping his teeth trimmed. ▷

Sociable gerbils

Gerbils like company, so it is best to keep two or more together. But beware: Gerbils that are strangers fight and can even kill each other. A male and female gerbil kept together will produce babies very quickly. So gerbils that are going to share a cage must be either all brothers or all sisters.

Black-patched gerbils starting to fight

Gerbils from the same litter will be friends. ▷

The burrowers

Gerbils need to be able to burrow and tunnel if they are to be happy. They can be kept in cages with wire bars, but a "gerbilarium" is the best home for them. This can be made from a fish tank. It gives plenty of room for the 6 inches (15 cm) of burrowing material they need, and you can watch them through the sides of the tank.

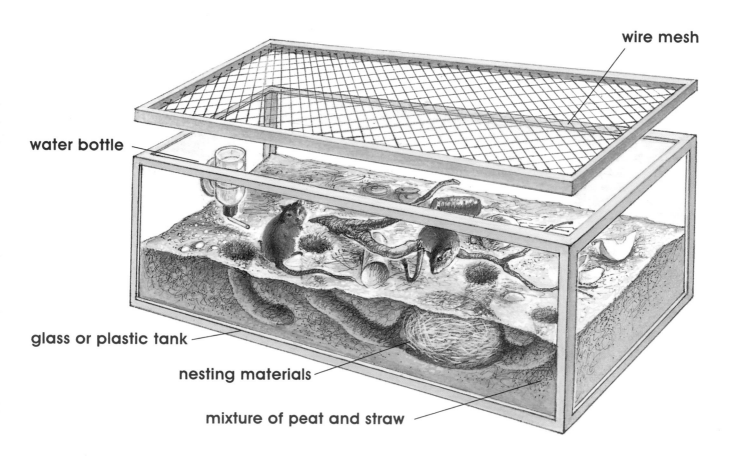

wire mesh

water bottle

glass or plastic tank

nesting materials

mixture of peat and straw

Mongolian gerbils asleep in a burrow ▷

Newborn gerbils

Gerbil parents stay together for life and the father helps to care for the family. The babies are born 24 days after mating. As the parents can produce another new family every 24 days, it is sensible to separate them in captivity. There are usually four or five babies, and they are born blind and hairless. It is important not to disturb them for the first few days.

Newborn gerbils are about 1 inch (3 cm) long

These Egyptian gerbils' fur appeared when they were five days old. ▷

Growing up

Baby gerbils grow up very quickly. They start to explore the nest when they are only a week old, although their eyes won't open until the tenth or twelfth day. They drink milk from their mother until they are four weeks old. After that they are ready to go to new homes. Gerbils are fully grown at three months.

Three-week-old babies start eating grains.

Young Egyptian gerbils playing ▷

Handle with care

Gerbils are nervous little creatures, so it is worth taking the time and trouble to make friends with them. One hand must always support the gerbil's weight when it is lifted. A gerbil can be gently picked up by the base of its tail, but never by the tip. If the gerbil "freezes" with fright, put it back in its cage.

This argente gerbil is being lifted correctly

20

Gerbils like funny places to hide in. ▷

Know your gerbils

A few pet shops sell Egyptian gerbils, but most pet owners keep Mongolian gerbils. There is a variety of different colored Mongolian gerbils to choose from. Select your pet carefully. You can recognize a healthy gerbil by its bright eyes, glossy coat, and its inquisitive nature.

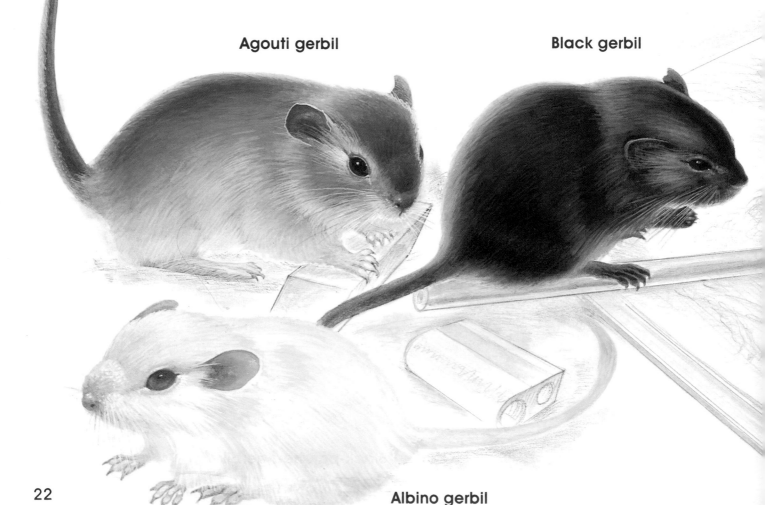

Agouti gerbil

Black gerbil

Albino gerbil

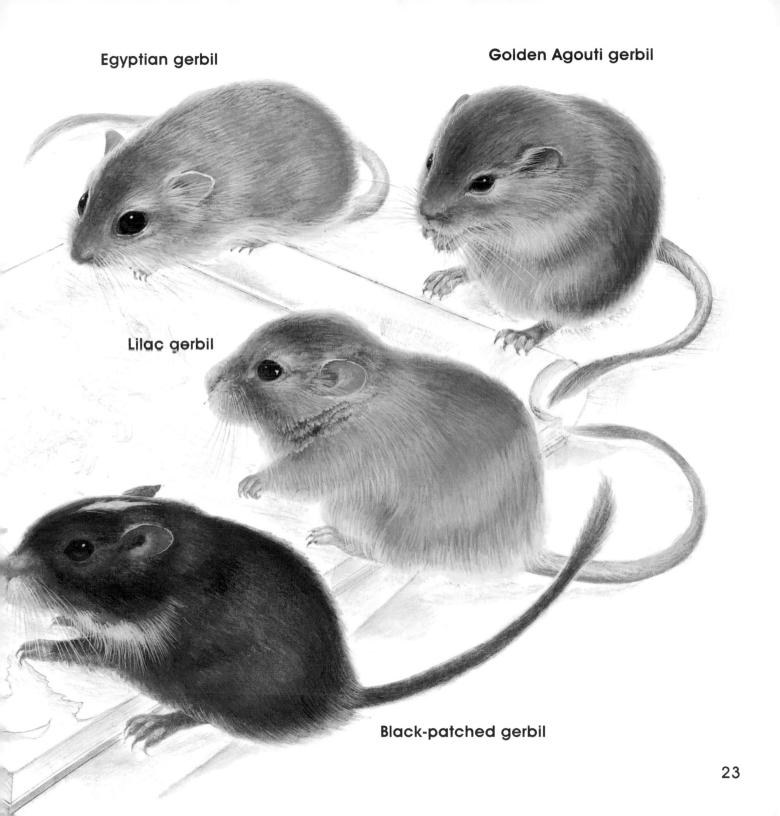

Egyptian gerbil

Golden Agouti gerbil

Lilac gerbil

Black-patched gerbil

Index

Photographic credits:

All photographs supplied by Bruce Coleman Ltd

Design	David West Children's Book Design
Illustrations	George Thompson
Picture Research	Cee Weston-Baker

First paperback edition for the United States and Canada published 1995 by Barron's Educational Series, Inc.

First published in the United States 1989 by Gloucester Press.
© Aladdin Books Ltd 1988

All inquiries should be addressed to:
Barron's Educational Series, Inc.
250 Wireless Boulevard
Hauppauge, NY 11788

Library of Congress
Catalog Card No. 94-26049
International Standard
Book No. 0-8120-9081-0 (paperback)

Library of Congress Cataloging-in-Publication Data

Petty, Kate.
Gerbils / Kate Petty; [illustrations, George Thompson].
p. cm.– (First pets)
Includes index.

Summary: An introduction to gerbils for one interested in that animal as a pet.
ISBN 0-8120-9081-0

1. Gerbils as pets–Juvenile literature. [1. Gerbils.] I. Thompson, George, 1994- ill. II. Title. III. Series: Petty, Kate. First pets.

SF459.G4P47 1995
636'.93233–dc20   94-26049
                         CIP AC

PRINTED IN BELGIUM

3456 987654321